Nickel Investing for Beginners

Roggie Clark

Learn How To Invest in Gold Bars With This Book

Whether you're new to investing or seeking to diversify your portfolio, this beginner-friendly guide will give you the knowledge and confidence to invest in gold, and other precious metals.

https://www.amazon.com/Ultimate-Investing-Buying-Guide-Beginners-ebook/dp/B0F1KWWDXG

Learn How To Invest in Physical Silver With This Book

Whether you're approaching retirement or already enjoying it, protecting and growing your wealth is critical. The Ultimate Silver Investing & Buying Guide For Beginners is your clear, no-nonsense guide to incorporating silver into your wealth-building strategy.

https://www.amazon.com/Ultimate-Silver-Investing-Buying-Beginners-ebook

Learn Macro and Micro Economics, With This One Book

Whether you're a student, a professional, or simply someone eager to understand the world around you, this book is your perfect introduction to the fundamentals of micro and macroeconomics.

https://www.amazon.com/Macro-Micro-Economics-Made-Beginners-ebook/dp/B0DPHTFVQG

Copyright

Title:Nickel Investing for Beginners
Author: Roggie Clark

Cover Design: Roggie Clark
Editing: Renee' Clark

Printed in the United States of America

Disclaimer

The views and opinions expressed in this book are those of the author and do not necessarily reflect the official policy or position of any individual, company, or organization cited or referenced in the text.

The author is not affiliated with any of the individuals, companies, or organizations mentioned in the text, nor does the author receive any form of compensation for citing or referencing them. Some sample scenarios in this text are fictitious. Any similarity to actual persons, living or dead, is purely coincidental.

The professional information (strategies, tips, and concepts) in this text is provided on an "as is" basis, without warranties of any kind, express or implied. While every effort has been made to ensure the accuracy of the information contained herein, neither the author nor the publisher makes any representations or warranties regarding its completeness, reliability, or applicability. The information is for educational and informational purposes only and should not be interpreted as professional, legal, financial, or business advice.

This book does **not** constitute financial advice, investment guidance, or legal counsel. Any financial, business, or investment decisions made based on this book are done **at your own risk**. You should always conduct your own research and consult a **certified financial**

advisor, legal professional, or other qualified expert before making any decisions that could impact your finances, business, or legal standing.

Neither the author nor the publisher guarantees any specific results or outcomes. By reading this book, you acknowledge and agree that the author and publisher shall not be held liable for any direct, indirect, incidental, or consequential damages, financial losses, or harm arising from the use or misuse of the information contained in this text. You assume full responsibility for any actions taken based on the content of this book.

Table of Contents

Introduction

Nickel is not usually the first metal investors think about. It does not carry the monetary mystique of gold, and it does not have the stacking culture of silver. But nickel plays a critical role in the modern economy, and that role is becoming more visible as global demand shifts toward electrification, infrastructure expansion, and advanced manufacturing.

Understanding nickel as an investment requires a different mindset than precious metals investing. This book is designed to provide that clarity.

Why Nickel Deserves Investor Attention

Nickel strengthens stainless steel. It supports infrastructure projects. It plays a central role in electric vehicle battery chemistry. It contributes to renewable energy systems and global manufacturing supply chains.

Unlike metals that are primarily monetary in nature, nickel's value is tied directly to industrial demand. When construction increases, when manufacturing expands, when electric vehicle production accelerates, nickel demand often rises alongside it.

That connection to real economic activity makes nickel structurally important. It also makes it cyclical.

Nickel Is an Industrial Commodity First

Gold is often purchased as a hedge against inflation. Silver serves both monetary and industrial purposes. Nickel is different.

Nickel moves primarily with global industrial output, infrastructure spending, and battery demand. During economic expansion, nickel demand can surge. During economic slowdowns, demand can contract quickly.

This is not a flaw. It is the nature of industrial commodities.

If you approach nickel expecting safe haven stability, you will misunderstand it. If you approach it as pure speculation without understanding supply and demand, you may underestimate the cycle behind it.

The key is perspective.

What This Book Will Cover

This guide will break down nickel from the ground up. We will examine where nickel comes from, how it is mined and processed, and which countries dominate global supply. We will analyze how electric vehicle demand and battery chemistry influence long term projections.

You will also learn the different ways investors gain exposure to nickel, including mining stocks, ETFs, futures contracts, and diversified commodity funds. Each method carries different levels of complexity, volatility, and risk.

Most importantly, we will discuss structure.

Nickel investing is not about chasing price spikes. It is about understanding the industrial cycle, the supply chain, and the macroeconomic forces that influence pricing.

The Reality of Commodity Volatility

Nickel is a commodity. Commodities are volatile.

They can rise sharply during demand surges. They can decline rapidly during global slowdowns. They can remain flat for extended periods while supply and demand rebalance.

Unlike dividend paying stocks, nickel does not produce income. Unlike real estate, it does not generate rent. Its value is derived from industrial necessity and global consumption patterns.

Entering this market without understanding volatility is a mistake. Entering it with structure changes the experience entirely.

Who This Book Is For

This book is written for beginner investors who want to understand base metals in a practical way. It is for those looking to diversify beyond traditional asset classes. It is for readers interested in electrification trends and industrial growth, but who prefer structure over speculation.

It is not written for short term traders seeking leverage tactics. It is not written for those expecting guaranteed upside.

It is written for disciplined learners.

Last Thoughts

Nickel may not receive the attention that gold and silver receive, but it sits at the intersection of industry, energy transition, and global supply chains. That position creates both opportunity and volatility.

The difference between speculation and strategy is understanding.

Before allocating capital, you should understand the structure of the market, the forces that drive demand, and the risks that shape price movement. That is what we will build in the chapters ahead.

Chapter 1: What Is Nickel and Why It Matters

Nickel is a naturally occurring metallic element used primarily for strengthening alloys and enhancing corrosion resistance. It is hard, ductile, and resistant to oxidation. These physical properties make it extremely useful in industrial applications.

But nickel's importance is not just chemical. It is economic.

Understanding what nickel is and how it is used is the first step toward understanding how it behaves as an investment.

The Industrial Backbone of Stainless Steel

Roughly two thirds of global nickel production is used in stainless steel manufacturing. Nickel increases strength, durability, and resistance to corrosion. Without nickel, stainless steel would not perform the way modern construction, medical equipment, transportation systems, and industrial machinery require.

This alone makes nickel deeply connected to infrastructure and global development.

When construction expands, when factories increase production, when emerging markets build cities and transportation networks, nickel demand often rises in parallel.

It is not speculative demand.
It is functional demand.

The Growing Role in Electric Vehicle Batteries

Nickel's importance has expanded beyond traditional industrial use.

Modern lithium ion batteries, particularly those used in electric vehicles, often contain nickel in their cathode chemistry. Higher nickel content in batteries can increase energy density, which improves vehicle range.

As governments encourage electrification and automotive manufacturers scale EV production, nickel demand from the battery sector has grown significantly.

This demand is not uniform year to year. It depends on battery chemistry trends, technology shifts, and government policy. But the direction of long term electrification has brought nickel into strategic conversations at the national level.

This introduces a new layer of demand volatility and opportunity.

Global Supply Concentration

Nickel supply is not evenly distributed across the globe.

Major producers include Indonesia, the Philippines, Russia, and Canada. Indonesia in particular has become a dominant force in recent years due to its significant reserves and expanding refining capacity.

Supply concentration matters.

When production is heavily concentrated in certain regions, geopolitical decisions, export restrictions, environmental regulations, or political instability can impact global availability.

Commodity markets respond quickly to perceived supply risk.

Understanding where nickel comes from helps investors understand why prices may react sharply to policy announcements or disruptions.

Mining and Processing Complexity

Nickel is not mined and sold in a uniform form.

There are different types of nickel deposits, including sulfide deposits and laterite deposits. These require different extraction and processing methods. Processing can be energy intensive and capital intensive.

Some nickel is produced as a primary product. Some is produced as a byproduct of other mining operations.

Production costs vary depending on ore quality, location, environmental regulations, and infrastructure.

When prices fall below production cost for higher cost producers, supply may tighten over time. When prices rise significantly, new projects may become economically viable.

This supply response is not immediate. Mining projects take years to develop.

The lag between price signals and production response contributes to commodity cycles.

The Commodity Cycle

Nickel behaves within a broader commodity cycle.

During global expansion phases, industrial demand increases. Supply may struggle to keep up in the short term, pushing prices higher.

As prices rise, new investment flows into mining and processing capacity. Eventually, increased supply can overshoot demand, leading to price correction.

During economic contraction, demand weakens. Prices decline. Higher cost producers may reduce output.

Over time, supply and demand rebalance.

This cycle repeats, though never in identical form.

Investors who understand the commodity cycle approach nickel differently than those who view price charts in isolation.

Why Nickel Matters to Investors

Nickel matters because it sits at the intersection of infrastructure, industrialization, and electrification.

It is tied to:

Global manufacturing growth.
Energy transition policies.
Battery technology evolution.
Emerging market development.
Supply chain geopolitics.

Unlike precious metals that may respond strongly to monetary policy, nickel responds more directly to industrial demand and supply constraints.

That makes it sensitive to economic growth projections, government stimulus programs, and manufacturing data.

For investors, this means nickel exposure is effectively a position on industrial momentum and electrification trends.

It is not monetary insurance.
It is industrial participation.

Last Thoughts

Nickel is not glamorous. It is not a safe haven. It is not a collectible asset.

It is a structural industrial input with growing strategic relevance.

Its price is shaped by global production, battery demand, infrastructure spending, and supply concentration.

If you want to invest in nickel, you must understand these drivers first.

Price charts tell you what happened.
Supply and demand tell you why.

With the foundation of what nickel is and why it matters established, the next step is understanding how you can actually gain exposure to it as an investor.

Now let's examine the different ways to invest in nickel.

Chapter 2: The Different Ways to Gain Exposure

Understanding what nickel is and why it matters is only the first step. The next question is practical: how can you actually invest in it?

Unlike gold and silver, nickel is not widely available in small physical formats for retail buyers. You will not find one ounce nickel coins in coin shops or commonly traded nickel bars in standard bullion markets. Most nickel trading occurs at the industrial level, which changes how investors gain exposure.

Because of this structure, most retail investors participate indirectly rather than through physical ownership.

Physical Nickel Ownership

In theory, physical nickel ownership is possible. In practice, it is inefficient and uncommon.

Nickel is primarily traded in large industrial quantities. Futures contracts represent significant tonnage, and industrial users purchase nickel in bulk for manufacturing. The value density of nickel is also far lower than gold or silver, meaning large physical volume is required to represent meaningful capital.

Storage becomes inefficient quickly. Liquidity becomes limited. There is no widespread retail resale network comparable to precious metals markets.

For these reasons, physical nickel ownership is rarely the most practical option for beginners. The logistics alone often outweigh the benefits.

Nickel Mining Stocks

A more common route is investing in companies that produce or explore for nickel.

Mining stocks provide indirect exposure to nickel prices. When nickel prices rise, revenue and profit margins for producers may expand, which can support stock price appreciation. However, the relationship is not perfectly linear.

Mining companies introduce additional variables beyond the commodity price itself. Management decisions, cost structures, debt levels, operational efficiency, labor issues, environmental regulations, and geopolitical risks all influence performance. Many nickel producers also mine other metals such as copper or cobalt, meaning their revenue streams are diversified across multiple commodities.

This can be beneficial for stability, but it also means stock performance may not track nickel prices precisely. Mining stocks offer operational leverage to commodity prices, but they also carry company specific risk that pure commodity exposure does not.

Exchange Traded Funds and ETNs

Exchange traded products provide another avenue for exposure. These instruments typically track nickel futures contracts or broader industrial metal indexes and trade like stocks through brokerage accounts.

For beginners, ETFs and ETNs are often the most accessible method. They eliminate the need to manage storage or analyze individual mining company balance sheets. However, they come with structural considerations that investors should understand.

Many commodity ETFs gain exposure through futures contracts rather than physical holdings. This introduces concepts such as contango and backwardation, which can affect performance over time. In certain market conditions, rolling futures contracts forward may create drag on returns.

Liquidity, expense ratios, and tracking accuracy also vary between products. While these instruments simplify access, they are not identical to owning physical metal.

Futures Contracts

Nickel futures trade on major commodity exchanges and provide direct exposure to price movement. Futures allow investors to speculate on future nickel prices with standardized contracts and margin requirements.

This route offers the most direct form of price participation, but it also introduces leverage. Leverage amplifies both gains and losses, and futures contracts require active management, including monitoring expiration dates and maintaining margin balances.

For beginners, futures markets can be complex and unforgiving. They are tools designed for experienced participants who understand contract mechanics and risk management.

Broad Commodity Funds

Some investors prefer broader commodity exposure rather than concentrating solely on nickel. Diversified commodity funds may hold a basket of industrial metals, energy products, and agricultural commodities.

In this structure, nickel represents one component among many. This reduces single commodity volatility but also limits direct impact from nickel specific price movements.

For investors seeking general industrial exposure without committing to a single metal, this approach can offer balance.

Choosing the Right Exposure Method

The best exposure method depends on your objective.

If your goal is relatively straightforward price exposure with minimal operational analysis, an exchange traded product may make sense. If you are comfortable evaluating company fundamentals and geopolitical risk, mining stocks may offer upside potential beyond the underlying metal price.

If you want broader commodity diversification, multi metal funds may provide smoother participation in the industrial cycle.

The mistake many beginners make is choosing an investment vehicle without understanding what truly drives its performance. Exposure method shapes risk profile, volatility, and potential return characteristics.

Before allocating capital, clarify what you are trying to achieve.

Are you positioning for electrification growth? Seeking cyclical industrial exposure? Diversifying beyond equities? Each goal may justify a different structure.

Last Thoughts

Nickel investing is less about finding a single perfect vehicle and more about understanding tradeoffs.

Physical ownership is impractical for most retail investors. Mining stocks introduce company level risk. ETFs introduce structural considerations tied to futures markets. Futures contracts introduce leverage and complexity. Diversified funds reduce concentration but dilute impact.

There is no universal answer.

There is only alignment between method and objective.

In the next chapter, we will go deeper into what actually moves nickel prices so you can better understand how these investment vehicles respond under different market conditions.

Chapter 3: Physical Nickel — Pros, Cons, and Practical Considerations

When investors think about metals, physical ownership often comes to mind first. Gold coins. Silver bars. Tangible assets stored in a safe.

With nickel, the situation is very different.

Before assuming physical ownership is an option, it is important to understand how nickel is traded and why retail access is limited.

Can You Own Physical Nickel?

Technically, yes.

Practically, it is difficult.

Nickel is primarily traded in industrial formats. Standard contracts on commodity exchanges represent large tonnage, often measured in metric tons rather than ounces. Industrial users purchase nickel in bulk for manufacturing, not in small investment-sized bars.

Unlike gold or silver, there is no established retail bullion infrastructure for nickel. There are no widely recognized one-ounce nickel coins or standardized small investment bars with strong resale markets.

Even if you were able to acquire refined nickel metal, the logistics quickly become inefficient.

Value Density and Storage

One of the biggest practical challenges with physical nickel is value density.

Gold carries high value in a small amount of physical space. Silver requires more space, but still remains manageable for many investors.

Nickel is far less value dense.

To hold a meaningful dollar amount in nickel, you would need significant physical volume. That introduces storage challenges, security concerns, and potential transportation issues.

For most retail investors, the storage burden outweighs the benefits.

Liquidity Considerations

Liquidity is another concern.

Gold and silver benefit from global recognition and a broad retail resale network. Local coin shops, online dealers, and private buyers actively trade these metals.

Nickel does not have that ecosystem at the retail level.

If you owned physical nickel in small quantities, finding a buyer at a fair market price could be difficult. Industrial buyers transact in large volumes. Smaller amounts may face wider bid-ask spreads or limited demand.

Liquidity risk should always be considered before acquiring any physical asset.

Pricing Transparency

Precious metals markets provide clear spot prices and well-established premium structures. Nickel pricing, while transparent at the industrial level, is not structured for small retail transactions.

Without standardized retail products, pricing transparency becomes more complicated. Premiums may not be consistent, and resale discounts could be substantial.

This makes cost efficiency difficult to evaluate.

When Physical Nickel Might Make Sense

While impractical for most investors, there are niche scenarios where physical nickel ownership could make sense.

Industrial users may hold inventory as part of business operations. Large institutional participants may transact in bulk quantities aligned with exchange standards.

For the typical beginner investor, however, physical nickel ownership is rarely the most efficient path.

Comparing Physical Nickel to Precious Metals

It is helpful to contrast nickel with gold and silver to clarify expectations.

Gold is held as monetary insurance.
Silver serves both monetary and industrial roles.
Nickel is overwhelmingly industrial.

Because of this, physical ownership does not provide the same strategic benefit as holding precious metals for diversification or inflation protection.

Nickel's investment appeal lies in price exposure, not physical possession.

Last Thoughts

Physical nickel ownership is technically possible but rarely practical for retail investors.

Low value density, limited resale markets, storage inefficiencies, and lack of standardized retail products make it an unattractive option compared to other exposure methods.

Understanding this early prevents unnecessary complication.

Nickel investing is generally more efficient through financial instruments rather than physical metal.

In the next chapter, we will examine nickel mining stocks in detail and explore how company exposure differs from direct commodity exposure.

Chapter 4: Nickel Stocks and Mining Companies

For most beginner investors, nickel exposure begins with mining stocks.

Unlike physical nickel, which is difficult to acquire and store efficiently, mining companies are easily accessible through standard brokerage accounts. They trade like any other publicly listed stock and can be purchased in small or large quantities.

But investing in a nickel mining company is not the same as investing in nickel itself.

Understanding that distinction is critical.

How Nickel Mining Companies Generate Revenue

Nickel mining companies generate revenue by extracting ore, processing it, and selling refined nickel or nickel-containing materials into the global market. When nickel prices rise, the revenue per unit sold increases. If production costs remain stable, profit margins can expand.

This is why mining stocks often rise when commodity prices rise.

However, the relationship is not perfectly linear.

A company's profitability depends not only on nickel prices, but also on operating efficiency, cost structure, energy expenses, labor costs, environmental compliance, transportation infrastructure, and debt obligations.

Nickel price may rise, but if production costs rise faster, margins may not expand meaningfully.

Pure Play Versus Diversified Miners

Some mining companies are primarily focused on nickel production. Others produce nickel alongside copper, cobalt, platinum group metals, or other base metals.

This distinction matters.

A diversified miner may benefit from multiple commodity cycles, reducing dependence on a single metal. However, its stock performance may not closely track nickel prices if other segments of its business dominate revenue.

A more concentrated nickel producer may provide stronger correlation to nickel price movement, but it also introduces greater exposure to nickel specific volatility.

Neither model is inherently better. Each carries tradeoffs.

Jurisdiction and Geopolitical Risk

Nickel production is geographically concentrated. Indonesia, the Philippines, Russia, Canada, and Australia are major players. Political stability, regulatory frameworks, environmental policy, and export controls all influence production dynamics.

When investing in a mining company, you are also investing in the jurisdiction where it operates.

Changes in tax policy, mining royalties, environmental regulations, or export restrictions can materially impact profitability. In some cases, geopolitical tensions can disrupt supply chains or create sanctions risk.

Commodity exposure always includes geopolitical considerations.

Capital Intensity and Project Development

Mining is capital intensive.

Developing a new nickel project requires significant upfront investment in exploration, permitting, infrastructure, equipment, and processing facilities. These projects can take years to move from discovery to production.

During this development phase, companies may raise capital through equity issuance or debt financing. This can dilute shareholders or increase financial leverage.

If nickel prices fall during development, projects may become uneconomical before reaching production.

Investors should understand whether they are buying an established producer with operating mines or an exploration company with future potential but no current revenue.

Cost Curves and Margin Sensitivity

Every nickel producer operates at a different cost point on the global cost curve.

Lower cost producers can remain profitable even when prices decline. Higher cost producers may struggle during downturns but benefit disproportionately during price spikes.

Understanding where a company sits on the cost curve provides insight into its resilience during commodity cycles.

Margin sensitivity often explains why mining stocks can move more dramatically than the underlying commodity price. Small changes in price can significantly impact profitability, especially for higher cost producers.

Balance Sheet Strength

Commodity cycles are unpredictable. Strong balance sheets help companies survive downturns.

Companies with low debt, healthy cash reserves, and diversified revenue streams are generally better positioned to endure periods of low prices. Highly leveraged companies may face refinancing risk if commodity prices remain depressed.

Before investing in mining stocks, reviewing debt levels, cash flow stability, and capital expenditure plans is essential.

Volatility Compared to Nickel Itself

Mining stocks often exhibit greater volatility than nickel prices.

This is due to operational leverage, financial leverage, and investor sentiment. In bullish commodity environments, mining stocks may outperform the underlying metal. In bearish environments, they may decline more sharply.

For investors seeking amplified exposure to nickel price movements, mining stocks can provide that leverage.

But leverage increases both upside and downside.

Last Thoughts

Investing in nickel mining companies is not the same as investing in nickel itself.

You are buying exposure to management decisions, operating efficiency, cost structures, geopolitical risk, and capital discipline in addition to the underlying commodity.

Mining stocks can provide meaningful upside during strong nickel cycles. They can also underperform during downturns or operational setbacks.

Before purchasing shares, understand what drives company performance beyond the metal price.

In the next chapter, we will examine exchange traded funds and fund-based exposure, and how those vehicles differ from individual mining stocks.

Chapter 5: ETFs, ETNs, and Fund-Based Nickel Exposure

For many investors, exchange traded products offer the most straightforward way to gain exposure to nickel without evaluating individual mining companies or navigating futures contracts.

ETFs and ETNs trade on stock exchanges, can be purchased through standard brokerage accounts, and allow investors to allocate capital with relative simplicity. But while they appear simple on the surface, their structure matters.

Understanding how these products gain exposure is essential before investing.

Futures-Based Exposure

Many commodity ETFs do not hold physical metal. Instead, they gain exposure through futures contracts.

A futures contract is an agreement to buy or sell a commodity at a predetermined price on a future date. Funds that track nickel prices often hold these contracts and roll them forward as expiration approaches.

This introduces an important concept: the shape of the futures curve.

When futures prices are higher than current spot prices, the market is said to be in contango. Rolling contracts in contango can create a drag on returns over time. When futures prices are lower than spot, the market is in backwardation, which may benefit fund performance during contract rollovers.

Over long periods, this structural effect can cause ETF returns to differ from spot price movements.

For beginners, the key takeaway is simple: futures-based ETFs may not track nickel prices perfectly.

Single Metal Versus Broad Commodity Funds

Some exchange traded products focus specifically on nickel exposure. Others include nickel as part of a broader industrial metals or diversified commodity basket.

Single metal funds provide more concentrated exposure. If nickel prices rise sharply, these funds may reflect that movement more directly.

Broad commodity funds dilute nickel's influence. This reduces volatility but also reduces the impact of nickel-specific price movements.

Choosing between concentration and diversification depends on your investment objective. If you are positioning specifically for nickel demand growth, concentrated exposure may align better. If you are seeking general industrial commodity participation, broader funds may offer smoother performance.

Expense Ratios and Liquidity

Every exchange traded product carries an expense ratio. Over time, management fees reduce overall returns. While these fees may appear small annually, they compound over longer holding periods.

Liquidity also matters. Some nickel-focused funds may have lower trading volume than broader commodity ETFs. Lower liquidity can result in wider bid-ask spreads, which increases transaction cost.

Before investing, review fund size, trading volume, and expense structure. Accessibility does not eliminate due diligence.

ETNs Versus ETFs

Exchange Traded Notes differ from Exchange Traded Funds in structure.

ETNs are debt instruments issued by financial institutions. They promise to deliver returns linked to an underlying index or commodity. Unlike ETFs, ETNs do not hold assets directly. Instead, they rely on the creditworthiness of the issuing institution.

This introduces issuer credit risk.

While ETNs may track their underlying index more precisely in some cases, investors must consider the financial stability of the issuer.

Understanding this distinction prevents confusion later.

Tax Considerations

Commodity-based funds can have unique tax treatment depending on structure and jurisdiction. Futures-based funds may generate different tax reporting requirements compared to equity-based ETFs.

Investors should review fund documentation and consult tax professionals when necessary. While taxes should not drive strategy alone, ignoring structure can create avoidable complications.

Volatility and Investor Behavior

ETFs make commodity exposure easier. Ease of access can encourage reactive behavior.

Because these products trade intraday like stocks, investors may be tempted to respond to short term price movement more frequently than necessary. Nickel remains a cyclical commodity regardless of the vehicle used to access it.

The instrument may feel modern and convenient. The underlying volatility remains.

Last Thoughts

Exchange traded products provide practical access to nickel exposure for most beginners. They eliminate storage issues and reduce the need to evaluate individual mining companies. But they are not identical to owning physical metal, and they are not risk free.

Futures-based structures introduce roll effects. Concentrated funds amplify volatility. Diversified funds dilute exposure. ETNs introduce credit considerations.

The key is understanding what the fund actually holds and how it behaves over time.

In the next chapter, we will examine futures and options directly, and why leveraged exposure requires a different level of risk management.

Chapter 6: Futures and Options Explained

Futures and options markets sit at the core of commodity price discovery.

While most retail investors gain nickel exposure through mining stocks or exchange traded products, the underlying pricing mechanism for many of those instruments originates in the futures market.

Understanding futures does not mean you must trade them. It means you understand how the market functions beneath the surface.

What a Nickel Futures Contract Represents

A futures contract is a standardized agreement to buy or sell a specific quantity of nickel at a predetermined price on a future date.

These contracts trade on regulated exchanges. They allow industrial users to hedge price risk and allow financial participants to speculate on price movement.

Futures contracts are marked to market daily. Gains and losses are settled through margin accounts, not only at expiration.

For example, if nickel prices rise and you hold a long futures position, your account balance increases daily. If prices fall, losses are deducted daily.

This structure creates immediate feedback.

Leverage and Margin Requirements

One of the defining features of futures trading is leverage.

To control a large contract value, you do not need to deposit the full contract amount. Instead, you post an initial margin, which represents a fraction of total exposure.

Leverage amplifies both gains and losses.

A small percentage change in nickel prices can result in a much larger percentage change in account equity. This is attractive during favorable price movement and dangerous during adverse movement.

For beginners, leverage is often underestimated.

Volatility in nickel markets can be substantial. Leveraged exposure magnifies that volatility.

Contract Expiration and Rollover

Futures contracts have expiration dates. If you hold a contract to expiration, you may be required to settle financially or, in some cases, take delivery depending on contract terms.

Most financial participants close or roll their positions before expiration.

Rolling means selling the near-term contract and purchasing a later-dated contract. The pricing difference between those contracts depends on the structure of the futures curve.

As discussed previously, contango and backwardation influence the cost or benefit of rolling forward.

Managing rollover is part of futures strategy. It requires monitoring contract calendars and understanding how term structure affects performance.

Options on Nickel Futures

Options provide the right, but not the obligation, to buy or sell a futures contract at a specified price before expiration.

Call options allow participation in upside price movement. Put options provide downside exposure or hedging potential.

Options introduce additional variables:

Time decay.
Implied volatility.

Strike price selection.
Expiration timing.

While options can be used for strategic hedging or directional exposure, they add complexity beyond straightforward futures trading.

Without a solid understanding of option mechanics, beginners may find them difficult to manage.

Who Should Consider Futures

Futures contracts are typically appropriate for:

Experienced traders.
Institutional participants.
Industrial hedgers.
Investors with advanced understanding of leverage and risk management.

They are generally not the starting point for beginners exploring nickel exposure.

The ability to control large value with limited capital is appealing, but it demands discipline and risk tolerance.

Risk Management Considerations

Because futures are leveraged instruments, risk management becomes central.

Position sizing must reflect account size.
Stop-loss discipline must be clearly defined.
Volatility tolerance must be realistic.

Nickel prices can move sharply in response to geopolitical events, inventory announcements, policy shifts, or speculative positioning.

Leverage transforms moderate volatility into potentially severe account swings.

Without strict risk management, futures can quickly overwhelm capital.

Comparing Futures to Other Exposure Methods

Futures provide the most direct price exposure.

Mining stocks provide operational leverage.
ETFs provide structural exposure.
Broad funds provide diversified participation.

Futures provide raw price movement, amplified by leverage.

Each method reflects a different balance between simplicity and control.

For most beginners, understanding futures is more important than trading them.

Last Thoughts

Futures and options markets sit at the foundation of commodity pricing, including nickel. They offer powerful tools for hedging and speculation, but they demand knowledge, discipline, and risk tolerance.

Leverage magnifies outcomes. Expiration cycles require active management. Volatility is constant.

For beginner investors, futures are often best studied before being used.

Understanding how these contracts function enhances your overall understanding of nickel markets, even if your exposure ultimately comes through stocks or ETFs.

In the next chapter, we will step back from investment vehicles and examine the broader demand forces shaping nickel's future, including electric vehicles, industrial expansion, and global energy transition trends.

Chapter 7: Global Demand Trends, EV Batteries, and Industrial Use

Nickel demand is not static. It evolves with industrial development, technological change, and global economic priorities.

If you want to understand where nickel prices may face structural support or pressure over time, you must understand how demand is shifting.

While stainless steel remains the dominant use, new sources of demand are altering the long term outlook.

Stainless Steel Remains the Core Driver

Despite headlines about electric vehicles, stainless steel still accounts for the majority of global nickel consumption.

Stainless steel is used in construction, transportation equipment, food processing, medical devices, industrial machinery, and countless other applications. It resists corrosion and maintains structural integrity in demanding environments.

As developing economies industrialize and urbanize, stainless steel demand typically rises. Infrastructure expansion, housing development, and manufacturing capacity all require durable materials.

Because stainless steel production is so closely tied to economic growth, nickel demand remains sensitive to industrial cycles.

The Rise of Electric Vehicle Batteries

The most discussed demand shift in recent years has been the growth of electric vehicles.

Many lithium ion battery chemistries use nickel to increase energy density. Higher nickel content in cathodes can extend vehicle range and improve performance. As automakers compete to improve battery efficiency, nickel rich chemistries have gained attention.

Governments in North America, Europe, and Asia have introduced policies encouraging EV adoption, including subsidies, emissions regulations, and infrastructure investment. These policies influence battery production targets and, by extension, nickel demand projections.

However, battery technology is not fixed. Manufacturers continuously experiment with alternative chemistries to reduce cost or reliance on certain raw materials. Shifts toward lower nickel battery compositions can influence long term demand.

Nickel's role in electrification is significant, but it is part of a dynamic technological landscape.

Energy Transition and Infrastructure

Beyond EVs, nickel participates in broader energy transition efforts.

Renewable energy systems require corrosion resistant materials. Grid expansion, energy storage systems, and industrial electrification all depend on durable alloys.

As countries invest in modernization of infrastructure, nickel demand may benefit indirectly through increased industrial activity.

These investments often occur over multi year timelines, which can provide sustained demand support rather than short lived spikes.

Emerging Market Industrialization

Developing economies represent another structural demand component.

As countries expand manufacturing capacity, improve transportation networks, and build urban infrastructure, stainless steel consumption tends to increase. This, in turn, supports nickel demand.

The pace of emerging market growth can significantly influence global nickel consumption trends.

Slower global growth may temper demand. Accelerated industrial expansion can tighten supply conditions.

Demand Concentration and Cyclicality

It is important to recognize that while new demand sources are emerging, nickel remains concentrated in industrial use.

That concentration reinforces its cyclical nature.

During global slowdowns, stainless steel production can contract. EV sales growth may decelerate if economic conditions weaken. Infrastructure spending may face fiscal constraints.

Demand is not guaranteed.

Commodity markets reflect these cycles in pricing.

Long Term Versus Short Term Trends

Investors often confuse long term thematic growth with short term price movement.

Electrification and industrial expansion may represent multi decade trends. But nickel prices can still experience multi year downturns within those broader themes.

Supply expansion, technological substitution, currency fluctuations, and macroeconomic tightening can all temporarily suppress prices.

Understanding the difference between secular demand growth and cyclical volatility helps maintain perspective.

Interplay Between Demand and Supply

Demand trends do not operate independently from supply responses.

If long term demand expectations rise, capital flows into mining and refining capacity may increase. Over time, expanded production can rebalance markets.

Commodity markets constantly adjust.

Investors who assume demand growth automatically guarantees uninterrupted price increases misunderstand how supply responds.

Last Thoughts

Nickel demand is shaped by stainless steel production, electric vehicle battery growth, infrastructure investment, and emerging market industrialization. These forces create long term structural relevance.

But structural relevance does not eliminate cyclicality.

Nickel remains sensitive to global economic growth and industrial output. It participates in expansion and contraction cycles.

Understanding these demand forces allows investors to contextualize price movement. When prices rise sharply, demand acceleration may be a factor. When prices fall, demand moderation may be at work.

In the next chapter, we will shift focus to supply dynamics, production costs, and the risks that can disrupt the market from the other side of the equation.

Chapter 8: Supply Dynamics, Production Costs, and Market Risks

Nickel demand often receives the most attention, especially when electric vehicle production headlines dominate the news cycle. But supply dynamics frequently drive the most dramatic price movements.

Commodity markets tighten or loosen based on the balance between how much material is needed and how much is available. When supply becomes constrained, prices can spike rapidly. When supply expands aggressively, prices can retreat just as quickly.

Understanding supply structure is essential before investing.

Geographic Concentration of Production

Nickel production is not evenly distributed across the globe.

Indonesia has emerged as the dominant global producer in recent years, significantly increasing output through policy support and refining capacity expansion. The Philippines, Russia, Canada, and Australia also contribute meaningful supply.

When production is concentrated in a limited number of jurisdictions, policy decisions matter.

Export bans, environmental regulations, royalty adjustments, or geopolitical tensions can alter supply expectations overnight. Even announcements of potential restrictions can move prices before any physical shortage materializes.

For investors, geographic concentration introduces political risk alongside economic risk.

Ore Types and Processing Complexity

Nickel is extracted from two primary deposit types: sulfide deposits and laterite deposits. These deposit types require different extraction and refining processes.

Sulfide deposits are generally easier and less energy intensive to process, but they are less abundant in certain regions. Laterite deposits are more common in tropical climates but require more complex and energy intensive processing techniques.

The type of ore influences production cost, capital investment requirements, and environmental footprint.

Not all nickel production is equal. Cost structure varies widely across producers.

Production Costs and the Global Cost Curve

Commodity markets operate along a cost curve.

Some producers can extract nickel at relatively low cost. Others operate near the marginal cost of production. When prices fall below marginal cost for higher cost producers, those operations may reduce output or shut down temporarily.

Over time, this supply response can stabilize prices.

When prices rise significantly above production cost, new projects may become economically viable. Capital flows into exploration and development. Eventually, increased supply can soften prices.

This cycle does not occur instantly. Mining projects require years of development. But the cost curve helps explain why commodity prices rarely move in one direction indefinitely.

Energy and Environmental Constraints

Nickel production is energy intensive. Refining laterite ores in particular requires significant power input. Rising energy costs can increase overall production expenses, tightening supply if margins compress.

Environmental regulations also influence output. Governments may restrict mining permits, impose stricter emissions standards, or limit land use in sensitive areas.

These constraints can slow project approvals and reduce near term production growth, supporting higher prices if demand remains steady.

Inventory Levels and Exchange Stocks

Nickel inventories held on major exchanges provide one visible indicator of market balance.

When inventories decline rapidly, it may signal tightening supply conditions relative to demand. When inventories build, it may indicate oversupply.

However, exchange inventories represent only part of global availability. Private storage, long term supply contracts, and off exchange stockpiles also influence market balance.

Inventory trends often affect sentiment as much as fundamentals. A sharp drawdown can trigger price acceleration if traders anticipate shortage.

Geopolitical and Trade Risk

Because nickel is strategically important for industrial and battery applications, it has become entangled in broader geopolitical considerations.

Trade tensions, sanctions, and strategic resource policies can disrupt supply chains. Countries seeking to secure domestic battery production may implement export controls or investment restrictions.

These developments introduce unpredictability into global supply flows.

Commodity markets respond quickly to uncertainty.

Speculative Amplification

While supply fundamentals drive long term pricing, speculative activity can amplify short term moves.

If traders anticipate supply disruptions, they may build long positions in futures markets. If those expectations change, rapid liquidation can occur.

This can create sharp spikes followed by equally sharp corrections.

Investors using mining stocks or ETFs may experience amplified volatility during these periods, even if long term fundamentals remain intact.

Interaction Between Supply and Demand

The most important principle to remember is that supply and demand interact continuously.

Rising demand may tighten supply.
Rising prices may encourage new production.
New production may relieve tightness.

Weak demand may create surplus.
Surplus may pressure prices.
Lower prices may reduce output.

This feedback loop defines the commodity cycle.

Nickel does not move solely because of demand growth or supply constraints. It moves because of the balance between them at any given time.

Last Thoughts

Supply dynamics shape the volatility of nickel markets as much as demand trends do. Geographic concentration, production costs, energy inputs, environmental regulations, inventory levels, and geopolitical risk all influence availability.

When prices move sharply, supply expectations are often part of the story.

Understanding production structure allows investors to interpret market movement more clearly. Instead of reacting to price alone, you can evaluate whether underlying supply fundamentals have changed meaningfully.

In the next chapter, we will bring everything together and examine how to choose the right nickel investment strategy based on your goals, risk tolerance, and portfolio structure.

Chapter 9: How to Choose the Right Strategy for Your Goals

By now you understand what nickel is, how it is used, what drives demand, how supply dynamics create volatility, and the various ways to gain exposure.

The remaining question is not whether nickel matters.

It is whether nickel fits your portfolio, and if so, how.

Choosing the right strategy requires clarity about your goals, risk tolerance, time horizon, and overall asset allocation.

Clarifying Your Objective

Before selecting an investment vehicle, define what you are trying to accomplish.

Are you seeking long term participation in electrification and industrial growth? Are you diversifying beyond equities and traditional sectors? Are you adding cyclical exposure to complement defensive assets?

Nickel is not monetary insurance. It is not a fixed income substitute. It is not a stable dividend generator.

It is a cyclical industrial commodity.

If your goal is capital preservation with minimal volatility, nickel may not be the primary tool. If your goal is strategic exposure to industrial expansion and energy transition trends, nickel may deserve consideration.

Clarity of objective shapes everything that follows.

Matching Exposure Method to Risk Tolerance

Different exposure methods carry different risk profiles.

Mining stocks introduce operational and geopolitical risk in addition to commodity price risk. They can outperform during strong cycles but underperform during downturns.

Exchange traded products simplify access but may be influenced by futures structure, expense ratios, and liquidity considerations.

Futures contracts provide direct price exposure with leverage, but they demand strict risk management and tolerance for amplified volatility.

Broad commodity funds reduce concentration but dilute nickel specific impact.

There is no universal best method. There is only alignment between comfort level and exposure structure.

Position Sizing and Portfolio Balance

Nickel should rarely represent a dominant share of a diversified portfolio.

Because it is cyclical, allocation should reflect that volatility. A modest position can provide exposure to industrial growth without overwhelming overall portfolio stability.

Position sizing matters more than entry timing.

Even a well researched investment can create stress if oversized relative to total assets.

Diversification remains foundational. Nickel can complement equities, bonds, real assets, or precious metals, but it should not replace balanced allocation.

Time Horizon Considerations

Commodity cycles unfold over years, not weeks.

Short term price movements are often driven by speculation, currency shifts, or temporary supply disruptions. Long term performance reflects broader industrial trends and production responses.

If you are investing with a multi year horizon aligned with electrification and infrastructure development, short term volatility may be easier to tolerate.

If your horizon is short, commodity exposure may introduce unnecessary uncertainty.

Time horizon should influence exposure method and position size.

Avoiding Narrative Investing

The most common mistake beginners make is investing based on headlines rather than structure.

Electric vehicle growth stories may be compelling. Infrastructure spending announcements may create enthusiasm. Supply disruption headlines may generate urgency.

Narratives can be informative.

They can also distort judgment.

Before allocating capital, return to fundamentals. Has demand structurally shifted? Has supply meaningfully tightened? Has valuation become stretched relative to cost structure?

Disciplined investing requires filtering narrative through analysis.

Reassessment and Flexibility

Strategy is not static.

As economic conditions change, demand projections evolve, and supply capacity expands, your allocation may require reassessment.

If nickel prices rise sharply and your position grows beyond intended allocation, trimming may restore balance. If prices decline and fundamentals remain intact, incremental additions may align with long term objectives.

Flexibility within structure prevents rigidity.

Structure without flexibility becomes dogma. Flexibility without structure becomes reaction.

Last Thoughts

Nickel investing is not about predicting the next price spike. It is about understanding industrial cycles and positioning accordingly.

Demand trends, supply concentration, production costs, geopolitical risk, and speculative flows all interact to shape pricing. Exposure method determines how those forces affect your portfolio.

Choose your strategy based on your objective. Size your position responsibly. Align your time horizon with commodity cycles. Filter narrative through structure.

Nickel can serve a meaningful role in a diversified portfolio when approached with discipline.

Now we conclude by bringing together the broader lessons of this guide.

Conclusion

Nickel is not a headline metal.

It does not dominate financial television. It does not carry the historical mystique of gold. It does not generate the retail enthusiasm that sometimes surrounds silver or speculative technology stocks.

But it matters.

Nickel sits at the center of stainless steel production, industrial expansion, battery chemistry, and global electrification efforts. It is woven into infrastructure, manufacturing, and supply chains that support modern economies.

Understanding that role changes how you view it as an investment.

Throughout this book, we examined what nickel is, how it is produced, where supply is concentrated, and how demand evolves through industrial cycles and energy transition trends. We explored the different ways to gain exposure, from mining stocks to exchange traded products to futures contracts. We discussed volatility, production costs, geopolitical risk, and the realities of commodity cycles.

The goal was not to promote nickel.

The goal was to explain it.

Nickel is a cyclical industrial commodity. Its price moves with global growth, manufacturing activity, infrastructure spending, and supply constraints. It can rise sharply during demand surges. It can fall quickly during economic slowdowns. It is influenced by policy decisions, energy costs, currency movements, and speculative positioning.

It is not monetary insurance.
It is not guaranteed growth.
It is not immune to volatility.

When approached with unrealistic expectations, it becomes stressful.

When approached with structure, it becomes understandable.

For some investors, nickel may serve as targeted exposure to industrial expansion and electrification. For others, broader commodity exposure may make more sense. For many, a modest allocation aligned with long term objectives may be the most appropriate approach.

The key principles remain simple:

Understand the asset.
Understand the cycle.
Choose the right vehicle.

Size the position responsibly.
Reassess as conditions change.

Commodity investing rewards patience and discipline more than excitement.

Nickel will continue to evolve as technology advances and global demand shifts. Supply will adjust. Prices will fluctuate. Headlines will amplify both optimism and concern.

Your advantage comes from structure.

When you understand why prices move, volatility becomes information rather than intimidation. When you align exposure with objective, short term noise becomes less disruptive.

Nickel investing for beginners does not require prediction.

It requires clarity.

If you now see nickel not as a mystery metal, but as a structured industrial asset with identifiable drivers and manageable risk, then this book has done its job.

Continue learning. Continue evaluating. Continue aligning strategy with structure.

That is how disciplined investors approach any commodity.

www.ingramcontent.com/pod-product-compliance
Lightning Source LLC
LaVergne TN
LVHW022317200926
848481LV00004B/1370
* 9 7 9 8 2 9 5 6 6 8 3 9 5 *